Pyramids of the Sun and Moon

by Rachel Russ

The Mystery of the Pyramids

An old city lies in a valley. It is surrounded by mountains. Two massive pyramids tower over the city.

What is the story behind these great pyramids? Who made them and why?

The pyramids hold many secrets.

City Plan

The city from long ago is in Mexico. You can still visit it today.

Mexico

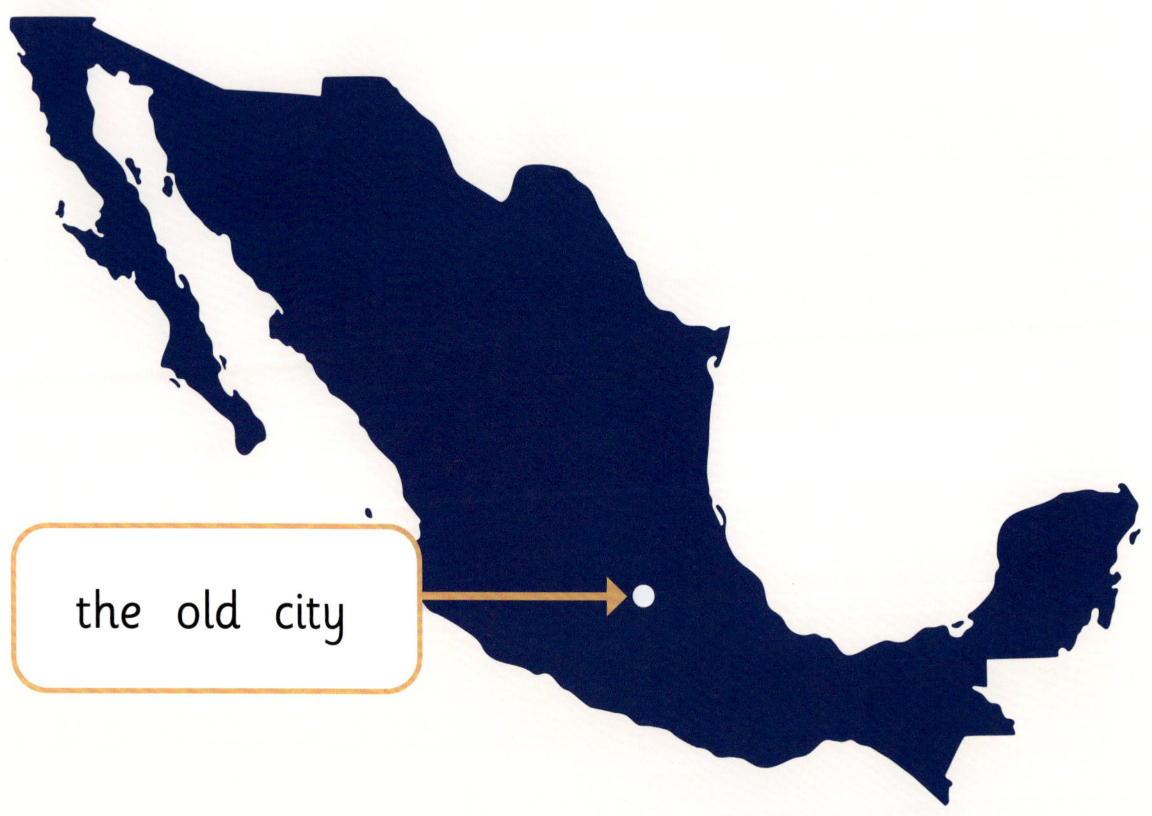

A long avenue connects the pyramids, homes such as **villas**, and important **monuments**.

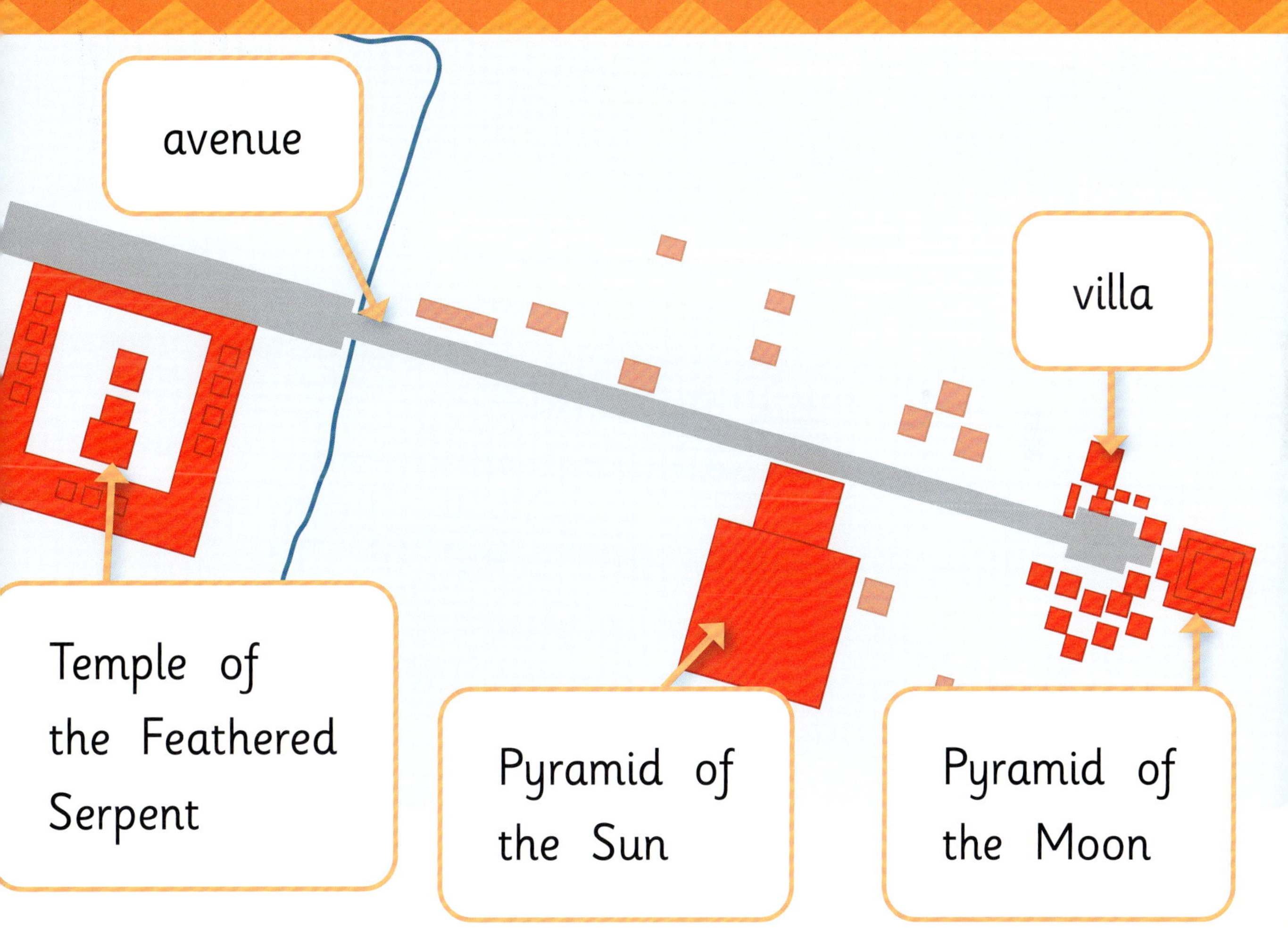

Pyramid of the Sun

The Pyramid of the Sun is tall. It is the third tallest pyramid in the world.

Over 200 steps lead to the top. Tunnels and caves lie underneath it.

There might once have been a temple at the top.

Pyramid of the Moon

At one end of the avenue is the Pyramid of the Moon. It is the second biggest pyramid in the old city.

This pyramid has steep steps!

There are lots of smaller pyramids around it. The graves of important **rulers** might be inside them.

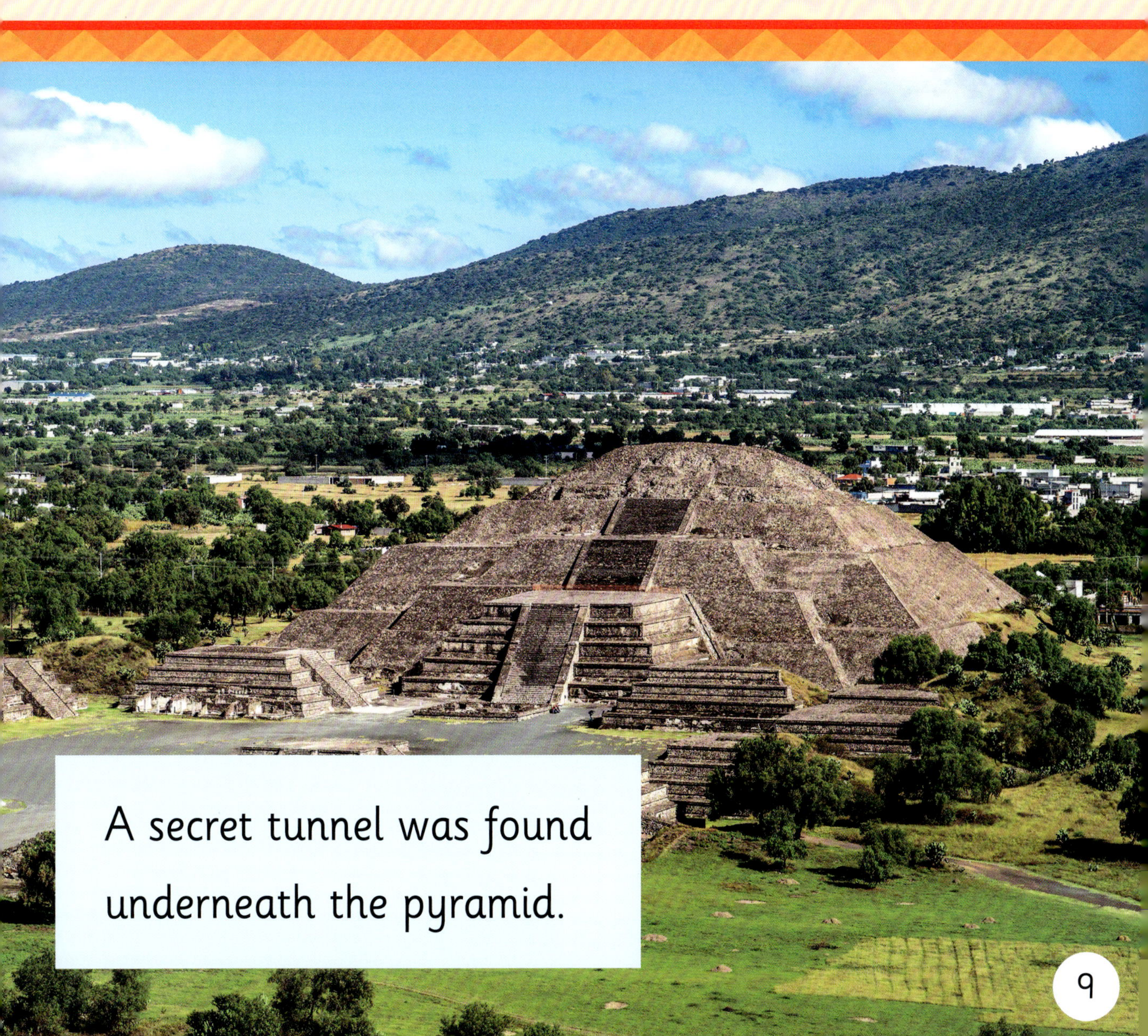

A secret tunnel was found underneath the pyramid.

Temple of the Feathered Serpent

This is the Temple of the Feathered **Serpent**. It is the third biggest pyramid in the old city.

The temple has amazing carvings on it. They show animals.

Inside, experts found masses of artworks.

The temple was full of interesting objects.

People of the Old City

Lots of people lived in the old city. Many stayed in apartments. Rulers lived in grand villas with **murals**.

Villa of the Butterflies

a grand villa mural

People grew crops such as beans to eat. They kept poultry, like chickens and turkeys. The people traded goods, such as pottery, with nearby cities.

Art and Valuables

Experts have **unearthed** many things in the old city. They have found items of great value. These include art and jewellery.

People prized green stone. This was because it looked like water. Water was important because it helped crops grow.

This necklace is made from green stone.

The city is decorated with murals. There are paintings of rulers. Many paintings show animals like pumas, eagles or snakes.

This painting shows a puma.

Statues were found in the city. This statue was carved from green stone.

Can We Solve the Mystery?

It is a mystery who constructed the old city. People came from many places to live there.

Why did people first come to the valley? Experts think people might have been fleeing from an erupting volcano.

After a long time, all the people left the old city. They left valuable items behind. Important monuments were burned. Why did people flee?

A group of people might have started a fire. Was it because they were angry with their rulers?

Experts are still trying to find out what happened.

The pyramids remain a mystery. There is so much still to learn.

What new things can the pyramids show us?

What secrets do the pyramids hold? Maybe one day the experts will solve the mysteries of the pyramids.

Glossary

constructed: made

monuments: important sites

murals: paintings drawn on walls

rulers: leaders such as kings, queens and emperors

serpent: a snake

unearthed: found; dug up

villas: grand homes

Index